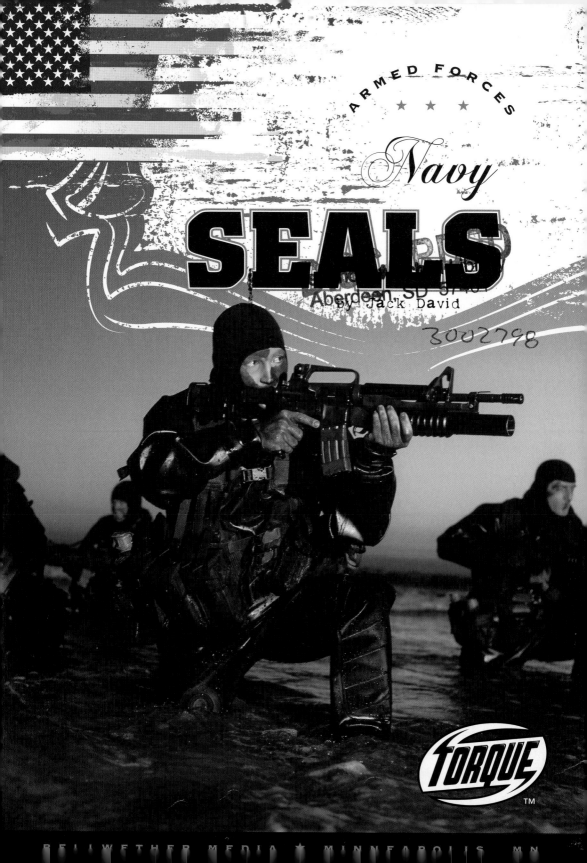

This edition first published in 2009 by Bellwether Media, Inc.

No part of this publication may be reproduced in whole
or in part without written permission of the publisher.
For information regarding permission, write to
Bellwether Media, Inc., Attention: Permissions Department,
Post Office Box 19349, Minneapolis, MN 55419-0349.

Library of Congress
David, Jack, 1968–
  Navy SEALs / by Jack David.
     p. cm. — (Torque. Armed forces)
  Includes bibliographical references and index.
  Summary: "Full color photography accompanies exciting
information about the Navy SEALs. The combination of high-
interest subject matter and light text is intended for students in
grades 3 through 7"—Provided by publisher.
  ISBN-13: 978-1-60014-265-9 (hbk. : alk. paper)
  ISBN-10: 1-60014-265-6 (hbk. : alk. paper)
  1. United States. Navy. SEALs—Juvenile literature. I. Title.
  VG87.D38 2009
  359.9'84—dc22   2008035643

Printed in the United States of America.

CONTENTS

★ ★ ★

★ ★ ★

Chapter One
WHAT ARE NAVY SEALS?

The SEALs formed in 1962. President John F. Kennedy wanted the Navy to have a special force similar to the U.S. Army's Green Berets.

The SEALs are an elite special operations force of the United States Navy. SEAL stands for Sea, Air, and Land. The SEALs can fight in any of these environments. They spend more than two years training to become the best fighters in the Navy.

SEALs go on a variety of **missions**. They seek out and destroy terrorists in **counterterrorism** missions. They carry out quick, surprise attacks on enemies or on enemy **assets** such as a military base or supply line. They go on **reconnaissance** missions to gather information about enemies or enemy territory. They plant explosives to destroy enemy ships and bases. Usually, enemies don't even have time to react before the SEALs get in, execute their mission, and get out.

SEALs have their own special war cry. "Hooyah!" is a way SEALs tell each other that they understand their orders.

Chapter Two
WEAPONS AND GEAR

The SEALs use a wide range of equipment. They carry guns, grenades, rockets, and other weapons. Depending on the mission, team members may each carry a different kind of weapon. All SEALs usually carry small handguns and larger rifles. They may also carry powerful automatic rifles such as the M14 and sniper rifles such as the M25. For armored targets, they may use a rocket launcher and an AT4 anti-tank rocket.

SEALs need other gear to complete missions. They often dive under water during missions. They have advanced **scuba** gear. Other SEAL gear includes **global positioning systems (GPS)**, long-range radios, **night-vision goggles**, parachutes, and climbing gear.

SEALs use two main types of scuba gear. Open-circuit gear uses tanks filled with oxygen. Close-circuit gear recycles the air SEALs breathe while underwater.

SEALs travel to missions in a variety of vehicles. The SEAL Delivery Vehicle travels just beneath the surface of the water so enemies cannot see it. Small boats carry SEALs from Navy ships to shore. Navy pilots may fly SEALs in with helicopters or planes.

SEALs sometimes use a simple boat called a rubber duck. This boat can even be launched from the air with the use of a special parachute.

Chapter Three

LIFE AS A SEAL

SEAL training is a long and grueling process that lasts more than two years. Only the smartest and most physically fit sailors can complete the training.

One of the most important parts of SEAL training is Basic Underwater Demolition/SEAL (BUD/S). BUD/S is split into three parts, or phases. They are Basic Conditioning, Diving, and Land Warfare. This training focuses on teamwork. Trainees learn to work together in high-stress environments. They also learn how to scuba dive in deep water, use parachutes, swim long distances, use weapons and explosives, **navigate**, and much more.

The hardest part of BUD/S training is called **Hell Week**. For five days and five nights, trainees are constantly training. They only get to sleep for four hours during the five-day training period. If they can't make it through Hell Week, trainees aren't fit to become SEALs.

Only about 25 percent of trainees successfully complete their training and become SEALs.

After their training, SEALs join their **platoons**. Each platoon has 16 members. SEALs are then divided into smaller **squads** or **elements**. Missions usually include only a few SEALs, and sometimes a SEAL performs a mission alone. SEALs are usually stationed on U.S. Navy ships. They're ready to carry out their missions on a moment's notice. With all of their training, they're prepared for almost anything.

GLOSSARY

★ ★ ★

asset—something of value to a military, such as a base, ship, or supply line

counterterrorism—a military mission designed to discover or prevent terrorist activity

element—a group of four SEALs within a platoon

global positioning system (GPS)—a device that uses satellites orbiting Earth to determine a precise position on the globe

Hell Week—an intense, five-day period of training in which SEAL trainees get a maximum of four hours of sleep

mission—a military task

navigate—to figure out position, course, and distance traveled

night-vision goggles—a special set of glasses that allow the wearer to see at night

platoon—a group of 16 SEALs

reconnaissance—secret observation

scuba—gear that helps divers breathe under water; scuba stands for self-contained underwater breathing apparatus.

squad—a group of eight SEALs within a platoon

TO LEARN MORE

★ ★ ★

AT THE LIBRARY

David, Jack. *United States Navy*. Minneapolis, Minn.: Bellwether, 2008.

Kaelberer, Angie Peterson. *The U.S. Navy Seals*. Mankato, Minn.: Capstone, 2005.

Yomtov, Nel. *Navy SEALs in Action*. New York: Bearport, 2008.

ON THE WEB

Learning more about the Navy SEALs is as easy as 1, 2, 3.

1. Go to www.factsurfer.com.

2. Enter "Navy SEALs" into the search box.

3. Click the "Surf" button and you will see a list of related Web sites.

With factsurfer.com, finding more information is just a click away.

INDEX

★ ★ ★

The images in this book are reproduced through the courtesy of the United States Department of Defense.